CW00683810

An Introduction to Poor Law Documents before 1834

SECOND EDITION

Anne Cole

Published by
The Federation of Family History Societies (Publications) Ltd
Units 15-16 Chesham Ind. Est., Oram Street, Bury, Lancs BL9 6EN

First published 1993
Reprinted 1996
Second edition 2000

Copyright © Anne Cole

ISBN 1 86006 127 3

Printed and bound by The Alden Group, London and Northampton.

Contents

Introduction

Poor Law records have become a major source of information for family historians for two reasons. Firstly, it is possible to prove relationships both between members of the same family and between families and places by using documents such as settlement certificates, settlement examinations and removal orders. Secondly, other Poor Law records, principally overseers' accounts, churchwardens' accounts and vestry minutes, can provide the means to follow pauper ancestors through their trials and tribulations.

It should not be assumed that these records are only of use to researchers with proven pauper ancestors. Those involved with local administration of the Poor Law were certainly not paupers for the various poor law documents and account books contain references to parishioners from all sections of society. It must also be remembered that a very large number of families lived from hand to mouth and relied on the good health of the wage earning members of the family for their day to day necessities. An accident such as a broken leg, or illness, could cause the family to become dependent upon poor relief, if only temporarily. A disaster such as a fire could put a well established tradesman out of business and make paupers of himself and his family. Poor law documents may be the only source of such information.

The Poor Laws touched almost every aspect of the lives of those who found it necessary to go cap in hand to the overseer of the poor as well as those whose predicaments drew them to the attention of the parish officers. The overseer of the poor was expected, when necessary, to feed, clothe, house and find work for his poor inhabitants. He apprenticed the pauper children and diligently sought, often with the aid of the parish constable, the fathers of illegitimate children born in his parish. Above all, he protected his parish from the claims of paupers who were not his responsibility. Much of the paperwork generated by all this activity has survived, with some counties having a far higher survival rate than others. The following pages will deal with the use and interpretation of these poor law records.

Where to find Poor Law Documents

The Diocesan or County Record Office is the most likely repository for poor law documents and all other parish chest material. However, some poor law information may be found in special collections at libraries. Some parish material may still be in the hands of the Parochial Church Council of the parish concerned. Record offices should have a list of all parish records that have not been deposited and this will include poor law documents.

Before visiting any record repository it is wise to establish whether the records you wish to consult actually exist. The amount of surviving poor law material differs very much from one county to another, and within the county, from one parish to another. For example, Lincolnshire has a very large collection of poor law documents whereas in Yorkshire very little poor law material has survived. Even in Lincolnshire there are a great many parishes where poor law records are non-existent.

Poor law documents may be listed with other parish records or separately as Civil Township records, especially in the north of England. Every record office has its own system of listing deposited material, and advice should always be sought when particular records cannot be found.

Quarter sessions records will also be found in record offices. Jeremy Gibson's guide *Quarter Sessions Records for Family Historians* gives a complete list of existing records, by county, including the location of the records and the existence of name indexes.

Indexes to poor law records for several counties or areas are in progress. Much of this work has been undertaken by Family History Societies, but record office staff and private individuals have also taken on this task. Many such indexes have been published and appear in the Federation of Family History Societies publications *Current Publications by Member Societies* which lists, in two volumes, publications in book form and on microfiche. *Specialist Indexes for Family Historians* by Jeremy Gibson and Elizabeth Hampson includes poor law indexes that may not have been published. It should be remembered that the accuracy of these publications relies on the co-operation of Family History Societies and their indexers. As indexes are updated the information contained in the booklets becomes out of date. The above publications should therefore be used as a guide and further inquiry should always be made to the Societies and indexers mentioned. Record offices may be able to advise about current projects concerning poor law documents.

The Parish Responsiblity

The offices of churchwarden and overseer of the poor were defined in the great Poor Law Act of 1601. Both were elected annually from the more substantial householders of the parish. The number of churchwardens and overseers in a parish varied considerably, some small parishes only having one overseer and one churchwarden, whilst many parishes in the north of England, being large and containing many townships, appointed overseers and churchwardens for each township.

Every parish was a self governing body, responsible for its own poor people. All the money needed for the care of the parish poor had to be raised by the parishioners and it was the parish officers' duty to collect this money by means of the poor rate. This system of parish government lasted until 1834 when the Poor Law Unions were created and responsibility for the poor passed to the Boards of Guardians of the various unions.

Apart from some overseers' and churchwardens' account books, few records survive from the early 17th century. The bulk of the poor law material which has survived dates from the 1680s as a direct consequence of an act of 1662 which founded the laws of settlement and removal.

A Place of Legal Settlement

The phrase "place of legal settlement" appears chiefly in settlement certificates, settlement examinations and removal orders. A person's place of settlement should not be confused with their place of birth or baptism. Neither should it be assumed that our ancestors always lived in their place of settlement.

The first Settlement Law of 1662 allowed any stranger to be removed from a parish if he did not pay £10 or more rent, or did not find security to indemnify the parish against any expense incurred on his or her behalf. Temporary visitors were obliged to provide a certificate from their own parish stating that they would be received back again. An act of 1691 laid down the ways in which settlement could be gained, and from 1697, people could move to a new parish provided they brought with them a Settlement Certificate.

The overseer of the poor had to deal with a new set of rules which enabled him to get rid of any paupers in his parish who had not settled there legally and were therefore not his responsibility. It became important that people should know what was their legal place of settlement and how they could gain a new settlement.

A legitimate child automatically took its father's place of settlement. However, the father's settlement was not necessarily the same as the parish in which the child was born. Any subsequent settlement gained by the father automatically passed to his wife and children. From the age of seven, children could be apprenticed and therefore begin the task of gaining a settlement for themselves.

A child apprenticed by the parish, or privately, who inhabited (i.e. slept in) a parish for 40 consecutive days under an apprenticeship indenture, could claim a settlement in that parish. By far the most common way of gaining a new settlement was by hiring and service. An agreement was made between master and servant, perhaps at an annual hiring fair (also called statute fairs) and provided the servant stayed the whole year with his master, until the anniversary of his hiring, leaving with his full wages, he gained a new settlement in the parish where his service took place. Boys, girls, or unmarried men and women may have gained a number of different settlements by service, each subsequent one replacing the former. A woman, on marriage, took her husband's place of settlement. This also applied to widows who remarried, any young children that she had by her first husband retaining their father's place of settlement whilst the woman took her new husband's place of settlement. Once married a man might rent a farm or smallholding, or set up as a tradesman in a new parish. If he paid £10 or more in annual rent, stayed the year and paid parish rates, he would gain a new settlement there. He might become a stalwart of the community and serve as a parish officer for a year, thus gaining a settlement in that way. Finally, a person who inherited or was given an estate in land, regardless of value, was able to claim a settlement in the parish in which the estate was situated provided that he lived on the estate for 40 days. However, a settlement gained in this way was made void if the person subsequently lived more than ten miles from the parish in which the estate was situated.

The legal settlement of an illegitimate child was the parish in which it was born. As overseers took great pains to remove pregnant single women to their places of legal settlement before the child was born, its parish of birth often coincided with its mother's legal settlement.

Settlement certificates, settlement examinations, removal orders and apprenticeship indentures all state the place of legal settlement of those concerned. Knowing an ancestor's place of settlement could lead to the discovery of new information about that ancestor in the records of a parish.

Poor Law Documents

Settlement Certificates

Whatever their shape and size and whether handwritten or printed, settlement certificates all share the same message:

> We the Churchwarden(s) and Overseer(s) of the parish of . . . do hereby certify, own and acknowledge that . . . (is or are) inhabitants legally settled in our parish of . . . (see figure 1).

The certificate goes on to say that the persons named would be accepted back in their parish of legal settlement provided that they had not gained a new settlement elsewhere.

A settlement certificate was a most important document to the person or family to whom it was given. It contained absolute proof of their parish of legal settlement, the only parish where financial help could be gained in times of need. At the same time, the overseer of the poor of the parish to which the certificate was brought could use the certificate as proof of settlement when removing unwanted paupers from his parish thus saving time and unnecessary expense.

The information given on settlement certificates varies. The most common printed form that appeared in the early 18th century leaves a large space for the names of those wishing to move from one parish to another. Unfortunately many overseers did not take advantage of this and simply wrote "John Smith and his family". This short statement could cover many eventualities. Perhaps John Smith was a single man and the overseer was looking ahead to the time when he would marry and have children. The words "if he hath any" are often added to the above statement. On the other hand the "family" may have included a wife, several children, and even other members of his family. In the latter half of the 18th century many certificates named the wife and all of the children, even giving their ages. Children described as "infants" could have been as old as seven years and very occasionally even older. The man's occupation may appear and, if he had an

Staff ss. WE *Henry Duncalfe Edmund Appley Jur.*
Cotton And Edw. Collins —

Church-Wardens and Overseers of the Poor of the Parish of
Penckridge — — — in the *County* of *Stafford*
aforesaid, do hereby own and acknowledge *Jn.º Wotton & Mary*
his wife and Children —

— — — — — to be, — Inhabitants
legally settled in the Parish of *Penckridge* — — —
aforesaid. In Witness whereof we have hereunto set our
Hands and Seals, the *22.ª* — Day of *May* — —
in the *13.th* Year of the Reign of our Sovereign *Lord*
George — by the Grace of God, of *Great Britain, France,*
and *Ireland, King* Defender of the Faith, *&c. Annoq; Dom.* 17 $\frac{27}{8}$
Church-Warden.

Attested by us
W.m Hodson
William Lee.

Henry Duncalfe
Edm. Appley

Overseers
John Cotton

To the Church-Wardens and Over-
seers of the Poor of the Parish of
Cannock in the County of
Stafford or to any or either of them.

Edw. Collins

WE whose Names are hereunto subscribed, Justices of
the Peace of the *County* — of *Stafford* —
aforesaid, do allow of the Certificate above-written. Dated
~~the~~ *Twenty seventh* Day of *May* — — *Annoq; Dom.* 1727

Jn.º Eginton
R.= Hun Back

Figure 1. The Settlement Certificate of Jn.º Wotton and his family from
Penckridge to Cannock, Staffordshire in 1727. (Courtesy of Staffordshire
County Record Office. Ref. D1054/7/15.

apprentice, his or her name would also be on the certificate. A man, his wife, their son and his wife and a grandson were all named on one certificate found in Lincolnshire.

Only children who were still dependent on their parents were included on settlement certificates. Many pregnant single women were given settlement certificates so that they could move, perhaps to be with their parents, before the birth of the child. The unborn child was included in the certificate and was therefore legally settled in the same parish as its mother regardless of where it was born.

A settlement certificate was issued by the overseers and churchwardens, and signed by two Justices of the Peace, but it is clear from settlement examinations that parishioners often had a say in who was granted a certificate. As the parishioners paid the poor rate, it is not surprising that they should decide who might be eligible to make a future claim for relief. If there was any doubt about a person's legal settlement, he or she would be examined by a magistrate, but an established member of the parish would have been well known and should have had no trouble obtaining a certificate. People often moved to a new parish without a certificate and requests were then made to their place of settlement for a certificate to be sent. The overseer or churchwarden often mentioned these requests in his accounts as the making of a certificate and sending it to another overseer was a small expense to the parish. It follows that the date on a certificate may not be the same as the date on which the bearer moved. Settlement certificates were not only used for paupers. Everyone from craftsmen and tradesmen to labourers were required to take with them a settlement certificate when they wished to remove to another parish.

It should always be remembered that the parish named on the certificate as the place of legal settlement is not necessarily the parish of birth, or former residence, of the bearer.

Settlement certificates were kept by the overseers in the parish chest. They have not always survived as inevitably some have gone missing over the years. Some overseers listed all their 'certificate men' in books specially kept for that purpose. The amount of information noted varies from place to place, but it is usual to find the name of the head of the family and the parish from which he came together with the year he arrived. Some overseers made lists of those arriving by certificate in parish registers, town books, or accounts books, anywhere they had a spare page to fill. References to 'a certificate man from . . .' may be found in baptism or burial registers. All such references should be followed up with a search of any poor law material from both parishes.

Settlement Examinations

Settlement examinations are by far the most informative of all poor law records (see figure 2). The examinant (as the person being examined was usually described in settlement examinations) was required to give evidence of how his legal settlement was gained and this was often accompanied by information irrelevant to that particular inquiry but of enormous value to family historians. Examinations survive from the early 18th century and were still being taken in some places in the 1860s.

Just how much detail was given in an examination depended on several factors, the most important being the way in which the legal settlement was gained. An examinant who gained a settlement by service or apprenticeship can be disappointingly silent about the rest of his life. Those who had not gained a settlement since their birth, however, were required to give more detail. A clerk who had spent all morning at the Quarter Sessions taking down the details of settlement examinations might be disinclined to note word for word the garrulous ramblings of a farm labourer giving his life story to the magistrate. Indeed, one examination in the Kesteven Quarter Sessions in Lincolnshire was reduced from two pages to a third of a page, the written statement of the examinant having survived. Unfortunately it is impossible to say how often this happened. There were, however, some clerks who were happy to include all kinds of irrelevant information, some of it often later crossed out but still readable today.

Sometimes several people were examined about one pauper. In some cases the parish officers went to enormous lengths to trace people who had been overseers or churchwardens of a particular parish up to forty years before in order to find evidence of the examinant's settlement. In cases such as these the details given about the informants can be just as important as those given about the examinant.

Many examinations are written on printed forms where space is provided for giving the examinant's age and place of birth. Although not always accurate, this information is perhaps the most useful. The way settlement was gained is dealt with next. The examinant may say at which statutes he was hired, by whom, the dates on which he began and ended his service, the parish in which he served and what his wages were. This is the only information pertinent to the inquiry but the approximate date and place of marriage, his wife's name and the names and ages of children are often added. The examiner was only interested in children who were still dependent on the pauper he was examining. It is possible that an examinant in his forties or fifties who stated that he had no children had actually brought up several children, all of whom had gained settlements of their own and were therefore independent of their parents. An examinant may have served several masters in subsequent years and all his services may be mentioned. If settlement was gained by apprenticeship, the relevant details will again be given, to whom apprenticed, his master's trade and parish, length of service etc. Where no settlement had been gained since birth the examinant would be required to give his place of birth, and often the name of his father (or mother and putative father if illegitimate) was given. Many paupers had rented houses and land, paid parish rates and served as parish officers. Different details would be given by these examinants; where and when land was rented and from whom, the amount of the yearly rent and often the cause of their present decline. Many married men were hired to work for farmers and details of wages and other 'perks' were given, such as how many cows their master allowed them and where they were allowed to graze.

Examinations were kept in the parish chest and have survived amongst the other poor law documents kept there. In some counties settlement examinations were also taken at Petty Sessions and may have survived. There are a very large number of settlement examinations of 'rogues and vagabonds' in certain Quarter Sessions records and these will be dealt with in a later chapter.

Parts of Lindsey a *The Examination* of William
County of Lincoln Douse now residing in the Parish of
Wainfleet all Saints in the said Parts
Labourer taken the ninth day of September
1835 before Joseph Flint Esquire one of
His Majesty's Justices of the Peace for
the said Parts

Who Saith I married my wife Ellen at Thorpe 16
years since the 2d of June last, the first place I lived
in for a year was with Widow Grayson of Great Steeping
who hired me on Spilsby Statute day 1807 for a year
from next May day without any agreement for a
Holiday and I served the year in Great Steeping in the
said Parts, I let myself the next Spilsby Statute day
to Mr William Brickhills of Hatton Holegate in the
said Parts Farmer for a year from the next May
day without agreeing for a Holiday and I served him
the year in Halton Holegate aforesaid, The next year
I let myself at Spilsby Statute to Mr John Ingstaff
of Bratoft for a year and bargained for a Holiday
I was to go home on the Sunday and return on the
Tuesday and I did so, The next year I let myself at
Leake Statute to Mr John Dawson of Friskney for a
year except a Holiday of three days and two nights
at Spilsby Fair which Holiday I had, In 1811 I let
myself to Mr Robert Betts of the East Fen for a year
except a Holiday from Sunday to Wednesday at
Spilsby Fair, and I had the Holiday. On Monday
before last I broke my Leg and arm through
falling from a Stack in the Parish of Wainfleet
Saint Mary's in the said Parts and I have done
nothing to gain a Settlement except as aforesaid
Taken and Sworn before me

Jos. Flint

William X Douse
        mark
his

Figure 2. William Douse gives details of several hirings in his examination
dated 1835. Opposite: Susanna Dennis adds further details about her
brother-in-law William Dowse. (Courtesy of Lincolnshire Archives. Ref.
Halton Holegate parish 13/6/7.

16

Copy

Parts of Lindsey ⎫ **The Examination** of Susanna
County of Lincoln ⎬ the wife of John Dennis of Wainfleet
‎ ⎭ All Saints in the said Parts Thatcher
taken on oath this fourteenth day
of September 1835 —

Who Saith, My Husband is Brother
to the wife of William Dowse of Wainfleet all
Saints aforesaid Laborer who lately broke his —
Leg And that the said William Dowse has two
Children by his said wife namely Edwin aged —
about six years and Algernon aged about four
years

Taken before us —

    Jos: Hunt

    J H Rawnsley.

                             her
                      Susanna ✕ Dennis
                          mark

        To Thomas Hardwicke Rawnsley Clerk

I Joseph Hunt do hereby certify the above —
examination to have been taken by me the —
day and year first above mentioned —

             Jos. Hunt

             J H Rawnsley.

Removal Orders

Any non-settled inhabitants of a parish could be removed back to their place of settlement if they became chargeable, or looked as if they might become chargeable, to the parish in which they were living. A removal order had to be signed by two Justices of the Peace and two copies were made, one for each of the parishes concerned. The fact that two copies were made and kept in two different parishes may have ensured a better survival rate for these documents.

Removal orders in the late 17th and early 18th centuries often give brief details of how the pauper's settlement was gained. They may give the name of the master for whom he or she worked, or to whom apprenticed. Later removal orders (which may continue up to the 1860s) give no such detail but they are often accompanied by settlement examinations. Removal orders from the late 18th century onwards give very specific information about those being removed. It is usual to find that all dependent children are mentioned, with their ages, and if some of the children had a different mother i.e. their father was married more than once, this might be stated. Children were often removed after their parents had died, or after one parent had died and the other absconded. Half-brothers and half-sisters (children of the same mother but with different fathers) could be removed to different places as each child took its father's place of settlement. A child older than seven years might have been separated from its mother if she had remarried a man with a different settlement to her first husband. A removal order might state that the husband was in prison (see figure 3) or had been transported; that one of the children named on the order was the illegitimate child of the wife born before their marriage. A woman's former husband together with his occupation and place of residence might be named. Where an illegitimate child was not born in the parish where its mother was legally settled, the laws of settlement could be strictly adhered to and the child removed away from its mother to the parish of its birth. A great many pregnant women were removed and they were usually described as such. More information might be gained about a family on a removal order for 1800 than can be gained from a 19th century census return.

County of Chester, to wit,

To the Overseers of the Poor of the Township of _Church_, _Dutton_ in the said County of _Chester_

WHEREAS you have made Complaint unto Us, whose Hands and Seals are hereunto subscribed and set, two of his Majesty's Justices of the Peace in and for the said County, That _Mary Duncalf (Wife of John Duncalf Labourer now a prisoner in the Custody of Matthew Henshaw Deputy Constable of the Castle of Chester) and Ellen their Daughter aged one Month or thereabouts_ —

have come to inhabit in your said Township, not having gained a legal Settlement there, and that _they are_ and we do adjudge _them_ to be actually chargeable to your said Township, contrary to the form of the Statute in such Case made and provided; AND whereas it appears to Us upon Oath, that the Place of the last legal Settlement of the said _Mary Duncalf and Ellen her Daughter_

is in the _Township_ of _Sutton by Frodsham_ in the _County of Chester_

THESE are therefore in his Majesty's Name to authorize require, and command you upon Receipt hereof, to remove and convey the said

Mary Duncalf and Ellen her Daughter

forthwith out of your said Township of _Dutton_ the next and directest Way to the _Township of Sutton by Frodsham_ aforesaid, in the said County of _Chester_ which we adjudge to be the Place of _their_ last legal Settlement, and to leave _them_ there, together with this Warrant, or a true Copy thereof, with the Overseers of the Poor of the _Township of Sutton by Frodsham_ aforesaid, who are hereby required to receive and provide for _them_ according to Law. Herein fail not at your Perils. Given under our Hands and Seals the _Seventh_ Day of _July_ in the Year of our Lord, one thousand eight hundred and _four_

Rich.ᵈ Richardson

Robᵗ Hodgson

Figure 3. This Removal Order, dated 1804, shows the kind of interesting detail that may be found. John Duncalf's imprisonment presumably led to his family's removal. (Courtesy of Cheshire Record Office. Ref. P28/5/12.

19

Those named on the removal order were not always removed immediately and were sometimes not removed at all. If a member of the family was too ill to be moved, or if a woman had just given birth, the removal was suspended until a later date. Many removal orders give this information on the reverse side of the document. It may be that a member of the family died as a result of the illness and this too would be noted when the surviving members of the family were eventually removed. In many cases, an agreement was made between the two parishes that the parish of settlement would undertake to maintain the family while they remained in the parish to which they had become chargeable. This made sense when it was possible for the pauper to earn a small amount of money by an occupation that could be followed in the latter parish but not the former.

When a family was physically removed, they were taken, perhaps by cart, with their possessions to their place of settlement, where they may have been provided with a house or lodgings. Most parishes had houses set aside for paupers, the rent being paid every six months by the overseer. Single persons may have walked to their place of settlement, or have been taken on horseback depending on the distance involved. The parish constable was often employed to make sure the pauper left the parish.

With the removal came the bill. If the overseer of the parish from which a pauper was removed had already given relief to the pauper, he would send his account to his opposite number in the pauper's parish of settlement and demand payment. These accounts often survive and amount to surprisingly large sums of money, especially if the pauper had been ill.

A parish could appeal against a removal order and notice of appeal had to be given before the next Quarter Sessions took place. The appeal was heard at the Quarter Sessions and the removal order was either confirmed or quashed.

Apprenticeship Indentures

A large number of pauper children were put out as apprentices by parish officers. Many were orphans and very young. Provided that they inhabited (slept in) the same parish for 40 consecutive days, and were bound an apprentice by Indenture, they could claim a settlement in that parish. To all intents and purposes the apprentice became a member of the master's family. If the master wanted to move to another parish, his apprentice was named on his settlement certificate. Likewise, if the master was removed back to his parish of settlement, the apprentice went too. The apprentice lived with his master throughout his apprenticeship and the master took on the responsibilities of a parent. If his master died, the apprentice could be re-assigned to another master by the parish officers. The apprenticeship could be cancelled by the mutual agreement of the apprentice, the master and the overseers, or by order of the Court of Quarter Sessions.

Masters could be chosen by the parish officers or by a ballot; in some places taking an apprentice was a duty attached to certain properties and in others the inhabitants simply took turns to take an apprentice. Refusal to take an apprentice was possible on payment of a fine. The parish paid for the apprenticeship, unless the child's parents could afford to pay some of the fee to which the parish would make up the difference. Two Indentures were made out on one piece of paper, one above the other, and signed by the overseer(s), the churchwarden(s), the master and two Justices of the Peace. The paper was then cut in half in such a way that when the two papers were fitted together they matched perfectly, and a forged indenture could not be used at a later date. One copy of the indenture was kept in the parish chest and the other was taken by the master who presented it to the apprentice at the end of his apprenticeship.

The indentures always gave the names of the apprentice and the master, and the parish to which the apprentice belonged (see figure 4). Other information that may be found includes the name of the apprentice's parents, his age, the parish of residence, the occupation of the master, and the trade or calling that the apprentice was to learn. The latter may differ from the stated trade of the master. Some indentures which survive from the early 17th century contain a fascinating list of things that the apprentice must not do, including playing cards and dice, fornicating or marrying without his master's permission. The master, on the other hand, promised to provide his apprentice with the necessities of life including food and drink, and,

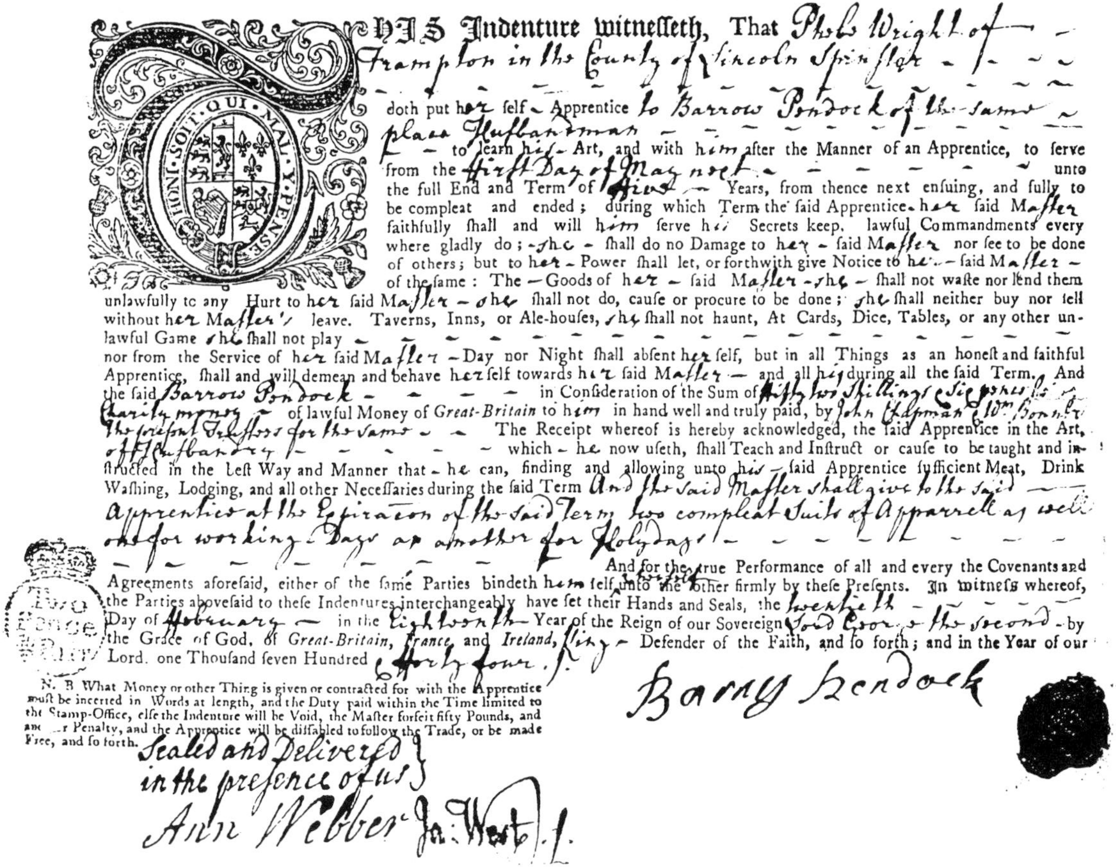
THIS Indenture witnesseth, That Phebe Wright of Frampton in the County of Lincoln Spinster doth put her self Apprentice to Barrow Pendock of the same place Husbandman to learn his Art, and with him after the Manner of an Apprentice, to serve from the first Day of May next unto the full End and Term of five Years, from thence next ensuing, and fully to be compleat and ended; during which Term the said Apprentice her said Master faithfully shall and will him serve his Secrets keep, lawful Commandments every where gladly do; she shall do no Damage to her said Master nor see to be done of others; but to her Power shall let, or forthwith give Notice to her said Master of the same: The Goods of her said Master she shall not waste nor lend them unlawfully to any Hurt to her said Master she shall not do, cause or procure to be done; she shall neither buy nor sell without her Master's leave. Taverns, Inns, or Ale-houses, she shall not haunt, At Cards, Dice, Tables, or any other unlawful Game she shall not play nor from the Service of her said Master Day nor Night shall absent her self, but in all Things as an honest and faithful Apprentice, shall and will demean and behave her self towards her said Master and all his during all the said Term. And the said Barrow Pendock in Consideration of the Sum of fifty two Shillings Sixpence being Charity money of lawful Money of *Great-Britain* to him in hand well and truly paid, by John Chapman & Wm Bonner the present Feoffees for the same The Receipt whereof is hereby acknowledged, the said Apprentice in the Art, of Husbandry which he now useth, shall Teach and Instruct or cause to be taught and instructed in the best Way and Manner that he can, finding and allowing unto his said Apprentice sufficient Meat, Drink Washing, Lodging, and all other Necessaries during the said Term And the said Master shall give to the said apprentice at the Expiration of the said Term two compleat Suits of Apparrell as well one for working Days as another for Holydays. And for the true Performance of all and every the Covenants and Agreements aforesaid, either of the same Parties bindeth him self unto the other firmly by these Presents. In witness whereof, the Parties abovesaid to these Indentures interchangeably have set their Hands and Seals, the twentieth Day of February in the Eighteenth Year of the Reign of our Sovereign Lord George the second by the Grace of God, of *Great-Britain*, *France*, and *Ireland*, King Defender of the Faith, and so forth; and in the Year of our Lord. one Thousand seven Hundred Forty four.

Barry Pendock

N. B What Money or other Thing is given or contracted for with the Apprentice must be incerted in Words at length, and the Duty paid within the Time limited to the Stamp-Office, else the Indenture will be Void, the Master forfeit fifty Pounds, and an...r Penalty, and the Apprentice will be disabled to follow the Trade, or be made Free, and so forth.

Sealed and Delivered in the presence of us

Ann Webber Jn: West

Figure 4. Phebe Wright was apprenticed to Barrow Pendock in 1744 to learn the Art of Husbandry. Her apprenticeship was for five years (Courtesy of Lincolnshire Archives, Ref. Frampton parish 13/7/80.)

usually, two suits of clothes, one suitable for Sundays. Until 1777-8 the apprentice served his master until he reached the age of 24, thereafter his apprenticeship ended at 21.

Many apprentices were to be taught a trade but others were not so lucky. The 'mystery and art' of husbandry, housewifery and women's business were very commonly stated as the 'trade' to be taught. Many children were simply used as servants in the houses of labourers and small farmers.

Some apprentices served masters who lived in the same parish as themselves, others were apprenticed outside the parish and thus gained a settlement elsewhere. Relatives were often named as the masters of pauper children. A second husband might take his wife's son by her first husband as an apprentice, thus ensuring that the whole family could claim the same place of legal settlement. Orphans were sometimes apprenticed to brothers or uncles.

Many apprentices suffered from ill-treatment at the hands of their masters. Some simply ran away but others took their cases to the Quarter Sessions and successfully prosecuted their masters.

The indentures of pauper children apprenticed by charities may also have survived in the parish chest. A rich benefactor of the parish might have left money to the parish with instructions that the money should be used to apprentice a certain number of pauper children each year. Children apprenticed by these charities appear to have been luckier than those apprenticed by the parish in that they were usually taught proper trades by their masters.

Parish apprenticeship indentures, some dating from before 1650, were kept with other poor law material in the parish chest. Some parishes kept Apprenticeship Books which give a little more information about the pauper and his family than the indentures may do. Solicitors may have administered charity apprenticeships, but many of these indentures have now been deposited in record offices.

Private apprenticeship agreements, that is where the family agreed with a craftsman or tradesman to take a son or a daughter as an apprentice, will not generally be found in record offices as the parish officers took no part in these arrangements.

Bastardy Documents

Bastard children were able to claim a settlement in the parish where they were born and parish officers did their best to try to ensure that bastard children were not born in their parish unless the mother could claim legal settlement there. If possible the putative father was apprehended well in advance of the birth, and made to pay the costs attendant on the birth and the maintenance of the child until it could be apprenticed or sent out to work. As soon as the mother was noticeably pregnant, or admitted that she was carrying a bastard child, the overseer went to work so that by the time the child was born several different documents recorded the details of the case.

The first stage in the process was to examine the mother to find out who the father of the child was. The *Bastardy Examination* may tell of the circumstances surrounding the conception as well as the name of the father. It may contain other small details such as the fact that the parents to be were both servants in the same household and the woman usually stated that she was promised marriage before the man had 'carnal knowledge of my body'. Not all the women were spinsters. Widows and married women whose husbands were or had been away, perhaps in the army, also gave birth to bastards. Some women were examined after the child had been born, whilst others, until the 1720s, were examined by midwives during the birth. The depositions of the midwife and her helpers may be found amongst some Quarter Sessions or Petty Sessions records. Where a woman was examined during or after the birth, the date of birth and sex of the child may also be given.

Once the overseer knew who the father was he could go to the next stage, which was to find and confront him with the woman's accusation. Sometimes the father, knowing what was coming, absconded and the overseer would then issue a *Bastardy Warrant* (see figure 5). Warrants were also issued after the birth of the child if the father did not keep up his maintenance payments. The sex and the precise date of birth of the child might be discovered on a later warrant. The fathers name, place of residence and sometimes his occupation should appear.

A *Bastardy Bond* may have been issued once the father was found and he had agreed that he was indeed the father. Bastardy bonds were

County of Lincoln,
Parts of
Lindsey

To the Constable of *Anderby* in the said parts.

WHEREAS Information hath been made unto us, two of his Majesty's Justices of the Peace in and for the said parts, one whereof is of the Quorum, and both of us residing next unto the limits of the parish Church, within the parish of *Anderby* in the said parts aswell upon the complaint of the Churchwardens and overseers of the poor of the said parish of *Anderby* — — — as on the Oath of *Esther Atra* — of *Anderby* — — aforesaid single Woman that on the *twenty third* Day of *August* — last past she the said *Esther Atra* — — was delivered of a *Female* bastard Child at *the House of John Ludly* in the said parish of *Anderby* — and that *William Tinker late* — — of *Maltby in the said parts* — is the father of the said bastard Child, and that the said bastard — Child is now living, and chargeable to the said parish of *Anderby* THESE are therefore to command you to bring the said *said Esther Atra* — before us at the ~~house of~~ *Justice Office in Alford* — in the said parts, on *Tuesday* the *Sixteenth* — Day of *November next* at the hour of Eleven in the forenoon of the same day to be by us further examined touching the Premises, and that you give notice to the said *William Tinker* — — — that he may likewise be and appear at the time and place aforesaid to make his lawful defence, to the end that upon the examination of the Cause, and Circumstance, we may take such order therein, as to right doth appertain; and what you shall do in the execution hereof, you are to make known unto us at the time and place aforesaid.

Given under our Hands and Seals the *Sixteenth* Day of *November* 1824.

W.H. Dashwood

J. Dodson

Figure 5. This warrant was issued after the birth of a female bastard child to Esther Atra. The constable of Anderby was commanded to take both Ester and William Tinker, the putative father, to be examined by a Magistrate. (Courtesy of Lincolnshire Archives. Ref. Anderby parish 13/13/1.

25

used throughout the 17th and 18th centuries and in some areas many early bonds have survived. The bond was an agreement between at least one bondsman and the parish of settlement of the mother stating that the parish of birth would be indemnified from all charges relating to the birth and maintenance of the child until it should die or reach seven years of age. Often the bondsman was the father, but this is not always stated. The name of the mother was given with the names, places of residence and occupation of the bondsman (or bondsmen). Occasionally a bond was entered into after the birth of the child and the child's name, age or date of birth may be given.

Once the child was born a *Maintenance Order* was made. The sex of the child was usually given, together with its date of birth and often in whose house the child was born. This is useful information as the child may have been born in a relative's home. The father was ordered to pay a named sum, being the costs of the birth plus a small sum, usually 1s 6d (seven and a half new pence) per week for as long as the child remained chargeable to the parish. The mother was also ordered to pay sixpence (two and a half new pence) a week in case she did not take care of the child herself.

If a father fell behind with his maintenance payments, or even absconded, the overseer would issue a warrant and once he was found a *Summons* would be delivered to him telling him to attend the next Quarter Sessions. The summons gave similar information to the warrant about the parties involved.

There are many bastard documents in Petty and Quarter Sessions records and these will be dealt with later.

As well as the poor law documents mentioned above, all kinds of other material may have been collected in the parish chest. There may be letters from one parish to another concerning settlement, apprenticeship or bastardy, or agreements made between parishes concerning the maintenance of various paupers. These cannot always be categorised but their possible existence should be noted.

Overseers' Accounts

As all the parish officers kept a careful note of the money they had spent the overseers' accounts are perhaps the most interesting. These books may survive from the early 18th century or even before. A good run of overseers' accounts for a parish will give the researcher an excellent insight into the day to day running of the affairs of the poor. In most cases the overseer was very particular about detail and noted every shoe, shirt and petticoat paid for (see figure 6). He did, of course, also note the recipients. Many paupers had their rent paid by the parish every six months. Other items they might have needed were clothing, fuel, flour, meat and medicine. The overseer paid doctors fees and funeral costs and he may even have paid for a modest wake. Some paupers received regular weekly payments and are often referred to as 'weekly pensioners'. It is interesting to see the cost of the various items in the 18th and 19th centuries. The overseer also noted his travelling expenses for journeys undertaken on behalf of the parish. He may have taken a woman to a magistrate to be examined about the bastard child she was expecting or perhaps he had to attend the Quarter Sessions to appeal against a removal order.

Money given to the mothers of bastard children was noted as were the payments made to him by putative fathers. If there is no other way of finding the name of a bastard child's father, an overseer's account book may hold the answer.

These accounts are littered with clues about the lives of the paupers concerned. Having read a few pages of an account book, the researcher will begin to recognise the tell-tale signs. Visits from the midwife and the doctor, payments for coffins, a new family being received from another parish, the overseer taking a young woman to the nearest town to 'father her child', or visiting one of his paupers in another parish, all clues to events in the lives of parishioners.

References to a pauper family should be sought in the overseers' accounts for the parish in which they were legally settled, regardless of where they resided. Paupers did not always live in their place of

The Disburisment of Joseph Challoner Overseer of the poor From the 4 of October 1807 to the 18 of April 1808 Being 28 Weeks

		£	s	d
	Pd Mr Flewiet on James Whitbeys Acct	0	10	6
14	Spent on Do 2 Jorney to Tarvin 16 —	0	4	2
	gave Thos Buckley — — —	0	3	0
	Pd for Brandey Oile and Sugercandy for Thomas Buckley —	0	4	0
10	Pd John Cranks Rant — — —	1	1	0
	Pd Bettey Burrowses Rent Northwich	2	2	0
21	gave John Lloyd — — — —	0	6	0
	Pd for a Letter from Stopart —	0	1	1
28	gave 7 Saylers with a pass — —	0	2	6
	gave Hannah penket to buy a Cow	2	0	0
7 Novbr	Thomas Buckley 25 Hundred of Coles 15 Carriage	1	0	0
	Sarah Burrows 23 Hundred of Coles & Carriage	1	3	0
	Hannah penket 22 Hundred Coles & Carba	1	2	0
	Pd for a payer of Shaws for Benets Lad —	0	4	6
9	Pd Emmats for Cloathing for Robats Lad at William Billington — —	0	15	0
30	To Mathew prince 25 Hundred & Carriage	1	10	2½
2 Decbr	margat Renchall 24 Ht Coles 17 Carriage	1	5	0
	gave mary Duggin — — — —	0	2	6
	gave Ralph Chesterses wife — —	1	0	0
5	gave Bettey Burrows to buy a Shift —	0	3	0
	gave Duncalfs Daughter to buy meat	0	2	0
	To gowing Wilberans and Northwich Spent	0	4	6
27	gave Joseph Shinglow for Rent — —	2	2	0
	Pd for a payer of shoas for Jos Forster	0	7	0
	Spent at a Towns meeting — —	0	7	0

Figure 6. Joseph Challoner's accounts for the months of October, November and December 1807 include 'Brandey Oile and Sugercandy for Thomas Buckley' worth four shillings. From the Little Budworth Township Overseer's Accounts. (Courtesy of Cheshire Record Office. Ref. P36/8/1.)

legal settlement and there may be few indications in the records of their parish of residence to show where their legal settlement was. It is entirely possible that a family could live and die in one parish whilst all the time being maintained by another parish with which they had no obvious connection.

Churchwardens' Accounts

The Churchwarden had fewer dealings with paupers than the overseer. He countersigned various poor law documents and took part in taking decisions about paupers but his accounts are more concerned with the parish ratepayers and the fabric of the church. A good set of churchwardens' accounts will give an annual listing of all the ratepayers in the parish, together with how much they paid. The poor rate was set each Easter at a Vestry meeting and the churchwarden then had the job of collecting the money.

His other duties involved the general welfare of the church and parish property. In his accounts will be found the names of the various tradesmen from whom he purchased items and the craftsmen he employed to do repairs to the church. It may have been necessary to buy a new church bell or provide musical instruments for the choir; all such items were noted in his accounts. He also paid parishioners for the mole heads and sparrows they brought to him. These were considered vermin and a small payment, usually one penny, was made for each mole or sparrow killed.

References to paupers in these accounts may be few and far between, although the churchwarden may have employed paupers to do menial paid tasks such as washing surplices or keeping the church clean. It is not uncommon, especially where the parish was small, to find that the churchwardens' and overseers' accounts are mixed up in the same volume. Here the researcher can kill two birds with one stone and find rich and poor alike on the same page.

Vestry Minutes

Vestry minutes are probably the most overlooked source for family historians seeking pauper ancestors. Today the vestry is the place where the minister and the choristers robe or 'vest' and where the spare flower vases are kept. At the time with which we are concerned however, the 'vestry' was a decision making body which took its name from the room in which it sat. There were two kinds of vestry, the open vestry, when the parish ratepayers attended, and the closed (or select) vestry, consisting of a small body of men, including the parish officers, elected by the parishioners. Meetings were held frequently, weekly or fortnightly in many parishes, and all the important decisions of the parish, especially those involving paupers and money, were made in the vestry.

At the Easter vestry meeting the parish officers, that is the Constable, Overseer(s) and the Churchwarden(s), were elected for a year. The rate to be charged by the parish officers was decided and any land belonging to the parish was auctioned to the highest bidder or leased for the following year.

A large variety of subjects were discussed at vestry meetings, mostly concerning pauper parishioners. The following list of items is from an early 19th century vestry minutes book from a small Lincolnshire parish: discussion about whether a boy should be put out as an apprentice; a doctor to examine a lunatic and report back to the meeting; an overseer directed to discover whether an appeal could be made against a removal order; a family were to be provided with a house and in the meantime the overseers were to obtain lodgings and bring the family into the parish; a discussion about how much relief a certain family was to be paid weekly and what clothes were to be supplied; it was agreed that a boy should be put out to service; a doctor was sent to see if a pauper could be cured so that he could work; the overseers were to take the necessary steps to prevent someone who had been removed from the parish from coming back; a man was to be sought who had left a son chargeable to the parish, the person who had been looking after the child to be paid; much discussion about a woman living in Sunderland, a certificate was sent and maintenance paid; a blacksmith applied to build a shop — request refused; certain people were to be taken into the workhouse; an inventory to be taken of the goods of someone who had become chargeable to the parish; discussion about building an extension to the workhouse; a vet was to be called to deal with a disease amongst horses in the parish; dogs were to be kept under control; a child was to be sent to school and the overseers were to pay for his books; discussion about innoculation for smallpox; someone's funeral expenses to be paid; nurses to be provided for sick paupers at 2 shillings a week; a musical instrument to be purchased for the use of the church choir.

The vestry minutes bring together all the parish issues in one book. Everything done by the overseer, the churchwarden and the constable was discussed first, and the whole parish, or its elected representatives, decided how the money was to be spent.

The survival of the vestry minutes, as with all other poor law material, is a hit and miss affair. There are unfortunately some parishes for which nothing from the parish chest has survived. If this is the case, the final resort must be to the Quarters Sessions records.

Workhouses

Workhouses were in existence long before the Poor Law Unions were created in 1834. One of the duties of the overseer of the poor, as defined in the 1601 Poor Law Act, was to find work for paupers, but the earliest workhouses were not set up until the end of the 17th century. These were buildings especially erected, purchased or rented, where paupers lived and were employed. There are many references in 18th century settlement examinations to people dying or being born in, or running away from, workhouses. Several parishes or townships may have shared a workhouse, and the expenses of keeping it in reasonable condition, whilst other parishes had no workhouse at all.

References to these workhouses may be found in overseers or churchwardens accounts, vestry minutes and Quarter Sessions records, as well as amongst other parish documents. These may contain details of repairs to workhouse buildings and payments made to paupers. Early maps or plans of parishes and towns may show workhouse buildings. Records concerning the day to day running of workhouses, and which mention the names of inmates, rarely survive.

Quarter Sessions Records

There are two sources for Quarter Sessions records, the files and the minute books. The files contain the actual documents collected at each sessions and may be in a fragile condition, very dirty and difficult to handle. There may be a separate file for each quarterly sessions, held at Epiphany (January), Easter (April), Midsummer (July) and Michaelmas (October), making four files per year to be searched. Poor law documents may be mixed up with all the other documents and may not be immediately recognisable as such. The minute books are far easier to search and often cover more than one year at a time. If possible, it is easier to find a case in the minute book before resorting to the files. Some minute books were indexed when full, but take care as these indexes may contain the names of the accused, but not the complainants. A putative father may appear in the index, but not the mother of a bastard child. Papers for many cases may not have survived in the files, or may not be available because of their condition, but where the documents have survived they may augment the information found in the minute book. The Quarters Sessions files for some counties have been microfilmed and are therefore available at Mormon Libraries.

The Quarter Sessions files are full of cases concerning paupers. The records are usually written in Latin until around 1700, and from then English is mainly used.

Rogues and Vagabonds

By far the largest collection of records of interest here are the settlement examinations and vagrancy passes for Vagrants and Rogues and Vagabonds. An act of 1743-4 described vagrants as persons threatening to run away and leave their dependents, those returning to a parish from which they had been removed and persons leading idle lives and begging in their own parish. Rogues and vagabonds were persons who wandered about begging, itinerant performers e.g. jugglers and minstrels, persons pretending to be

Egyptians (gypsies), fortune tellers, card sharps and other tricksters, unlicensed pedlars, persons who left families chargeable to a parish, who lodged in barns or in the open air and who were not able to give a good account of themselves, pretended soldiers or seamen and all other persons wandering abroad and begging. A third category, incorrigible rogues and vagabonds, was made up of persons who escaped from custody, refused to be examined, lied when examined and repeated a former vagrancy offence. Such people were apprehended by parish constables, often after a tip off from a parishioner, and were held in the local House of Correction until the next Quarter Sessions.

The vagrancy laws were applied rigorously across the country and a very large number of cases have survived in Quarter Sessions records. The vast majority of these cases however do not deal with performers, card sharps, or any of the other categories of people mentioned above. Many were simply people who, for one reason or another, were travelling when some misfortune befell them, or ran out of money and were forced to ask for relief. They include shipwrecked sailors, discharged soldiers, soldiers' wives and families returning home, runaway apprentices, legitimate travellers whose business had not turned out as planned, women whose husbands had left them or children whose widowed mothers had left them and who were attempting to return to their places of settlement, people who had travelled to find work and had fallen ill and people who were simply trying to get from one place to another and had become destitute on the way. All were examined and their examinations make fascinating reading. They came from all parts of the United Kingdom, from America and the West Indies, and from mainland Europe. Some of the 'pretended seamen' told fantastic tales of being captured by Moors, rescued and returned to England by Maltese ships. Some women had returned to their husbands' legal settlement to find another wife installed there. Some had suffered loss by fire and had licences to beg for charity. Others had passes given to them so that they could travel without being apprehended but still found themselves before the magistrates. Punishments such as whipping in a public place on market day were handed out to men and women alike. Many spent up to three months in the House of Correction before being sent to their place of settlement. Some examinants gave their age and place of birth, place and time of marriage, their wife or husbands name, even maiden names. Details appear about service, apprenticeship, soldiers' regiments and length of service, reasons for discharge, names of ships, countries visited etc.

With the examinations are the vagrancy passes stating where the rogues and vagabonds were to be sent. Whole families can be found as well as single men and women and often unaccompanied young children. Additional documents such as travel passes and testimonials may also be found. Some people who found themselves being apprehended for vagrancy appear to have taken the precaution of carrying with them a letter from a previous employer or an important member of their parish of settlement. The travel passes may contain a note of all the parishes through which the vagrant had passed on his way home, stating how he had been conveyed i.e. on horseback or on foot, and how much relief he had been given. Vagrancy examinations do not generally appear after 1820, but after that date many vagrancy convictions can be found, particularly for men who had run away leaving their families chargeable, or who refused to work.

Parish Appeals

A parish could appeal against a removal order and such appeals were heard at the next Quarter Sessions. Evidence would be taken about the pauper's place of settlement and the case would often be held over to the next sessions so that more evidence could be found. A copy of the removal order was kept with the other papers collected at the sessions and may be found in the Quarter Sessions files. Other documents collected at the time may include a settlement certificate or apprenticeship indenture, used in evidence at the time of the appeal. These may date from some years before the appeal was heard. There may also be an account of the expenses incurred by the overseer of the parish after making a successful appeal. The judgement will usually be found either at the bottom or on the reverse side of the removal order. The order would either be confirmed or vacated and discharged (quashed). There may be notes about small children who were to be sent elsewhere, or a reason may be given for the judgement. There were cases where the removal was quashed because the order had not been correctly written out. Settlement examinations may also be found. Where a removal order has not survived in the parish chest, it might be found in the Quarter Sessions.

Bastardy Papers
Removal orders may only appear in the Quarter Sessions where an appeal was made. Most bastardy cases, however, were automatically taken before the magistrates. Those few cases that do not appear were probably dealt with privately and may not be found in any official source. Many women were examined about the father of their child at the Quarter Sessions and the examinations will be found in the files. Putative fathers were ordered to attend the next sessions and to make sure that they did a recognizance (or bail bond) was entered into. The bondsman was usually, but not necessarily, the putative father, with a relative or friend appearing as his surety. Where the putative father was a minor a relative, often his father, would be the bondsman and the relationship between them was often stated. The mother was also named. Recognizances can be found in both the files and the minute books. Some counties had separate minute books containing recognizances, which were not only used for bastardy cases. Most recognizances were entered into before the birth of the child, but those dated after the birth may contain details about the child.

A calendar of prisoners, or a calendar of recognizances will be found in most sessions files. The father's name only may appear, but often the mothers name was added, together with their residences, or the name of the parish to which the child would become chargeable. The calendars continued to list the case until it was brought to a conclusion. The case may have taken several months and may appear in two or three consecutive sessions. These calendars usually give little detail but now and again a note may be made by the final appearance to the effect that the child was born dead, its parents had married, one of the parents had died or even that the woman was never pregnant.

Bastardy certificates may also be found in the files. Once the child had been born and the father had paid up, a certificate stating that the father had given sufficient security to the parish to which the child was chargeable, was sent to the magistrates. 18th century certificates may give details of the mother and the father, plus the sex of the child, and sometimes other information may be given. Later certificates may just state that 'a filiation order has been made' whilst giving little extra detail.

From the beginning of the 19th century, examinations after the birth began to appear. These gave the names of the parents, when and where the child was born, and the place of residence of the father which may be different from his place of residence given on an earlier document, especially if he was in service. These examinations were often accompanied by an account of the expenses incurred by the parish where the child was born (see figure 7).

The Quarter Sessions are unpredictable and differ considerably from county to county, but any kind of useful information may appear. There may be letters from parish officers stating that the child had not yet been born, or that the parents of a bastard child had married before the child was born. A putative father could appeal against a bastardy order made out against him, and often did. In such cases the bastardy order may be found along with warrants and summonses. The Quarter Sessions for Kesteven in Lincolnshire revealed the case of a bastard kidnapped by the father. A young man was accused of being the father of a child born to a known prostitute. When the overseer tried to bribe him to marry her, he took the overseer to court and won the case. A woman had hidden a dead bastard child in a box under her bed and the gory details of the inquest were found. Another woman pleaded for the return of her bastard child whom she said had been sold to gypsies by its father.

Maintenance Orders and Property Auctions

Not all paupers received relief from their parish of settlement. If it was found that a widow had a wealthy son, or orphan children a wealthy grandfather, the rich relative could find himself being ordered to maintain his poor dependents (see figure 8). Parish officers could also be ordered by the court to maintain a pauper whom they had hitherto refused to help. The amount the paupers were to receive would be given. These maintenance orders often appear in the

Thomas Ogden

1824	To the Parish of Wellingore	
Nov 17	Journey to Fulbeck with Sarah Whitaker to swear her child	4 · 0
18	Journey to Collingham to apprehend Thos Ogden	7 · 0
"	Expences same time	3 · 0
19	Journey to Broughton to bind Ogden to the Sessions	8 · 0
"	Expences same time	7 · 3
"	Expences at Newark and Buckingham	3 · 0
"	Paid Mr Moody for backing the Warrant	1 · 0
"	Paid Collingham Constable for apprehendg Thos Ogden	4 · 6
Decr 2	Expences of Sarah Whitakers lying in	1 · 0 · 0
"	Childs linen	10 · 0
31	Paid to the Child 1 Week	1 · 6
Jany 6	Do	1 · 6
"	Paid Doctors Bill for Midwifery	10 · 6
	Order	4 · 10 · 0
		13 · 6
		4 · 14 · 9

Lying in £ 2 · 3 · 0
Apprehendg ² 2 · 11 · 3
Order
4 · 14 · 9

Figure 7. These accounts, from the Kesteven Quarter Session, follow the progress of a bastardy case from the initial examination of Sarah Whitaker to the birth of her child. (Courtesy of Lincolnshire Archives. Ref. KSB Epiphany/1825/118B.)

39

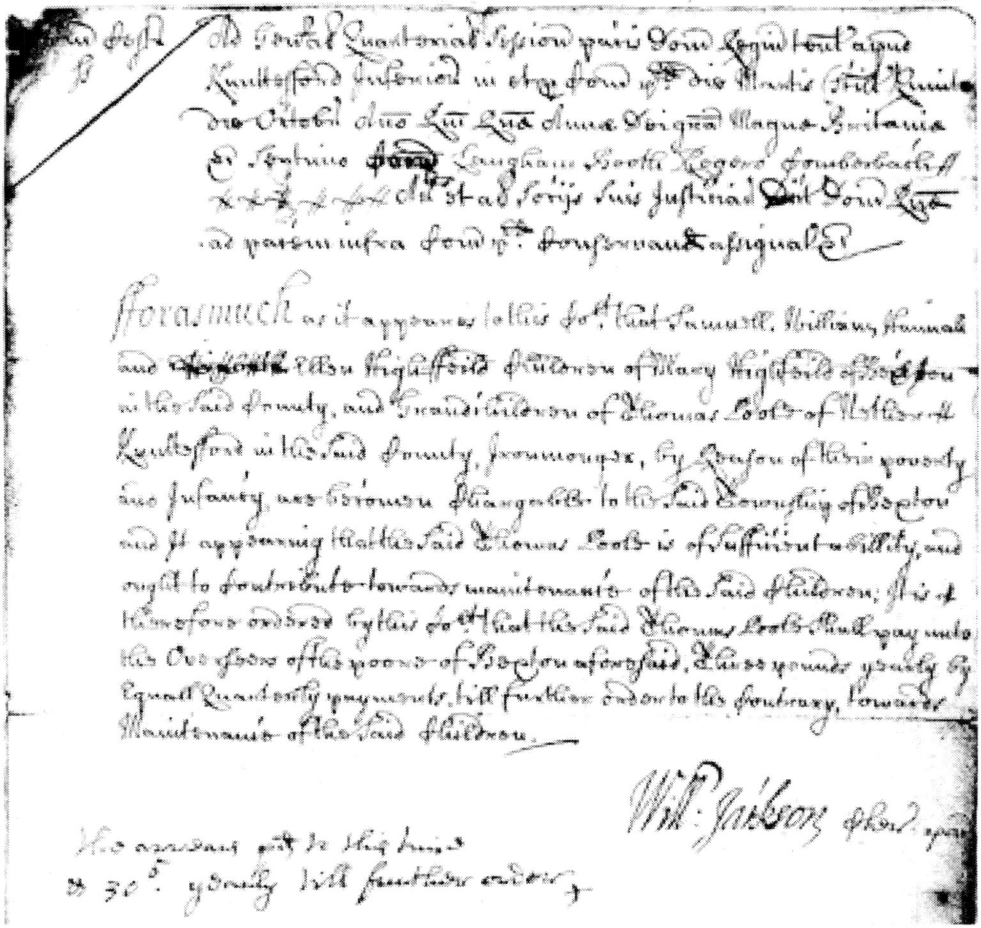

Figure 8. This maintenance order from the Cheshire Quarter Sessions dated 5 October 1810, orders Thomas Poole of Nether Knutsford, ironmonger, to pay £3 a year towards the maintenance of his grandchildren, Samuel, William, Hannah and Ellen Highfield, daughter of Mary Highfield of Bexton. (Courtesy of Cheshire Record Office. Ref. MF 212/173/QJF 147/2/27.)

Quarter Sessions, and they could give family details not to be found elsewhere, particularly in the 18th century.

When a pauper died leaving even a very small amount of property the overseer could recoup some of the money that the pauper had been given whilst alive by selling his household goods. An account of these sales sometimes appear in the Quarter Sessions files, but they may also be found with the parish chest material or in the overseers' accounts book.

Petitions

Amongst the large numbers of petitions in the Quarter Sessions files will be found petitions from people who have become paupers through an accident. Perhaps a business was lost through fire or some other natural calamity. The petitioner would ask permission to beg for charity in the neighbourhood, and would be given a document signed by the magistrates to say that he had this permission. Many such documents, carried by people who were picked up as rogues and vagabonds, were found to be forged. Masters could also petition to be rid of an unruly apprentice, or an apprentice might plead to be released from a master who ill-treated him.

Petty Sessions

Where Petty Sessions were held alongside Quarter Sessions the documents mentioned above, particularly bastardy papers, may be found in the Petty Sessions records. The existence of both types of record will differ from county to county in England and Wales.

Conclusion

There can be no doubt that poor law records should be seen as a major source for family historians. The information contained in the documents can solve many problems and an understanding of the laws of settlement and removal can lead to new avenues of approach to family history. However, researchers must be prepared to find a total lack of poor law material in many parishes, and a very poor survival rate in certain counties. Where the records have survived the researcher can enter the world of the pauper and the overseer thus gaining a deeper understanding of the world in which our ancestors lived.

Further Reading

The Parish Chest, W.E. Tate, Phillimore

English Local Government, VII, English Poor Law History Pt.1

The Old Poor Law, S, and B. Webb, 1929

The Old Poor Law 1795-1834, J.D. Marshall, Economic History
 Society, 1968

Poor Relief in England and Wales 1601-1834 , G.W. Oxley, 1974

Poor Law Statutes Vol. 1, J. Brooke Little, 1901

The Handy Book of Parish Law , W.A. Holdsworth, Esq., first
 published 1859, pub. Wiltshire Family History Society 1995

NOTES

NOTES

NOTES

NOTES